How to Write Better Book Reports

by Elizabeth A. Ryan

Jeff. L. J Sept 23,92

Troll Associates

Library of Congress Cataloging-in-Publication Data

Ryan, Elizabeth A. (Elizabeth Anne), (date)
    How to write better book reports / by Elizabeth A. Ryan.
        p.   cm.—(Student survival power)
    Summary: Presents faster and easier ways to do book reports.
    ISBN 0-8167-2458-X (lib. bdg.)   ISBN 0-8167-2459-8 (pbk.)
    1. Report writing—Juvenile literature.   2. Book reviewing—
Juvenile literature.   [1. Report writing.   2. Book reviewing.]
I. Title.   II. Series.
LB1047.3.R93   1992
372.6—dc20   91-3134

Contents

Introduction:
How To Use This Book

Why You Need This Book

One of the school assignments you will have to do most often involves writing a book report. All through middle school, junior high school, senior high school, and even college, teachers will want you to summarize the main points in books you have read. You will be asked to give your opinions of books and to decide whether to recommend them to others. In fact, many people make their livings writing *book reviews*—another name for book reports—that get printed in magazines and newspapers.

Because writing book reports will be such a big part of your schoolwork, you will find it helpful to learn faster and easier ways of writing them. After all, reading can be a lot of fun. Telling someone about what you read can also be enjoyable. The whole process will be easier to accomplish if you start with a clear idea of how to proceed, step by step.

This book will help you do that. We'll go through the whole business of writing book reports—from choosing a book that you'll want to read, through ways of reading that will make it easier to write your report later, down to putting together a first and then a final draft. By knowing what to concentrate on at each step, you'll be able to avoid that vague, nervous feeling that often goes along with having to write a report.

You may want to read this book straight through. That way, you can see for yourself all the different steps involved in writing a book report. When you actually write a report, you can follow the steps outlined in this book.

However, there may be only one or two parts of writing a report that are giving you trouble. In that case, you can use the Contents to help you. You'll see chapter headings on the different kinds of books there are, on how to get help from a librarian, and on what other resources you can find in the library. Decide in which area you need help, and turn to that chapter. If later you want to know about some other part of writing a report—such as how to take notes or how to revise a first draft—you can look in the Contents again.

Whether you read this book all the way through or in sections, there is one thing you should always remember while writing your report: *Take it one step at a time!* Don't worry about how you are going to finish your report while you're choosing a book from the library shelves. Don't interrupt your reading to wonder whether the teacher will like your report. Instead, focus on just what you are doing at the time—the next step will come soon enough. This book will help you break your report down into smaller steps so that you can give your full attention to each part of the process. Relax while you're working so that you can truly enjoy reading your book and telling other people about it.

Part I: CHOOSING A BOOK

Chapter 1:
What Kinds of Books Do You Like?
(Narrowing the Field)

Obviously, the first step in writing a book report is to choose a book to read. Of course, your teacher may already have assigned you a book or told you to choose one book out of a prepared list. But if you are allowed to choose one of your own, you might as well select one you will enjoy reading for its own sake.

Fact or Fiction?

There are many different types of books. One easy way to divide them up is into *fiction* and *nonfiction*. Fiction books are stories that are ''made up,'' that didn't actually happen. Romances, westerns, science fiction, ghost stories, mysteries, and novels are all called fiction.

Nonfiction books are supposed to contain ''facts,'' information that is not made up but can actually be proven. Nonfiction can also be a person's thoughts or opinions. A book about religion would be considered nonfiction. So would a book explaining how to fix a chair or work a video camera. Books about travel, science, space travel, odd facts, history, how movies are made, or the development of rock music would all be considered nonfiction. A *biography*, or the story of a real person's life, is considered nonfiction even though it might read like a made-up story.

What Do You Like To Read?

As you can see, there are many different types of fiction and many different types of nonfiction. Depending on your interests, you might enjoy several types of books. Here's some help in figuring out what might be a good book for you to read.

► Are you interested in space travel, other planets, or men from Mars? Do you like knowing about the stars and constellations? Are you fascinated by strange inventions and new gadgets? Do you read newspaper or magazine reports about the latest developments in the U.S. space program? Do you enjoy imagining what life might be like in the future?

If these topics interest you, you might like reading *science fiction*. Science fiction, as its name suggests, is fiction that "takes off" on scientific questions. *Star Trek* is an example of science fiction. Science fiction is often set in the future, as the author tries to imagine new developments in science and how they will affect our lives. A lot of science fiction concerns life on other planets, space travel, interplanetary warfare, and life in other worlds.

You might also enjoy nonfiction *science books*. If so, *astronomy*, the study of the stars and planets, would make enjoyable reading, as would books on *space travel* or on more offbeat topics, such as the sightings of *UFOs* (unidentified flying objects). There are also many nonfiction books about the *future*, in which scientists and others try to make predictions about what our society will be like by the time you grow up. *History of science* books, which tell how scientists through the ages have made their discoveries, might also interest you.

▶ Do you like solving puzzles and riddles? Are murder mysteries and police shows your favorite television programs? Do you like surprises in your reading? Have you ever thought that maybe you'd like to be a detective or a police officer, or thought about how interesting it might be to help solve a crime?

If so, you should have an easy time finding a book you like to read. *Murder mysteries* and *detective stories* are just made for you! There are many books featuring teenage or young adult detectives. You can also find adult detective stories that will interest you. If you've never read anything by Sir Arthur Conan Doyle, now might be a good time to start. Conan Doyle is the author who created the most famous detective of all—Sherlock Holmes.

If you're already a murder mystery fan, you might try branching out a little bit. Perhaps you would enjoy a nonfiction book about *real crimes* and criminals throughout history. You might be able to find a book about *famous unsolved mysteries*, or a book about *how police officers are trained* and how they do their work.

► Do you like love songs and romantic movies? Do you and your friends spend hours talking about girls or boys that you like, or keeping up with who's dating whom? Are you intrigued, puzzled, or fascinated by why and how people fall in love?

If you're answering yes to any of these questions, it sounds as though you might be interested in *novels about love and romance*. Many famous novels are love stories. Look at books like *Pride and Prejudice* by Jane Austen and *Jane Eyre* by Charlotte Bronte. *Wuthering Heights* by Emily Bronte is another famous love story that is also a great novel. You might also want to find young adult books in which the main characters—girls or boys—are figuring out dating, love, and romance.

Some of the greatest love stories can be found in history. Ask your teacher or librarian about *biographies* of some of history's famous couples, such as Queen Victoria and Prince Albert. You might also enjoy reading the biographies of romantic figures like Anna Pavlova, the ballerina, or perhaps the life stories of famous movie stars, actors, and actresses. If you want to think more seriously about love and relationships, you might look for *psychology* books that help explain why people act as they do.

► Are you fascinated by the idea of ESP (extrasensory perception)? Do you always read your horoscope in the daily paper? Have you always been interested in magic? Maybe you enjoy stories about witches, wizards, and warlocks.

If you feel drawn to fantasy and the supernatural, you will find plenty of books, both fiction and nonfiction, of interest to you. In the nonfiction section of the library, look for books about *psychic phenomena*, studies of ESP, or reports of famous "haunted houses" or puzzling events that no one has ever been able to explain. You might also want to look in the history section for books about the beliefs and *mythologies of other cultures*. Many cultures believed in magic, astrology, numerology, or the possibility of foretelling the future. Reading about the Greeks, Romans, Aztecs, Incas, Egyptians, or people of other ancient cultures might turn out to be fascinating. The spiritual beliefs of various African and Native American peoples might interest you as well.

Of course, there is also plenty of fiction on these topics! It's called *fantasy* and is usually found near the science fiction section of a library or bookstore. Fantasy writing can be set in another world or another time, but it can also be set in the ordinary world with a slight "twist." Some of the best fantasy writing for young adults is by Edward Eager. Ursula LeGuin is another fascinating writer of both fantasy and science fiction.

► Have you ever wondered how a television works or wished you knew more about computers? Do you like fixing things around the house, or wish you knew more about how to work with wood, cook, fix a car, or sew a shirt? Are you intrigued by trivia and offbeat facts? Do you like learning new skills? Do you enjoy remembering funny little pieces of information that no one else knows, like the way crickets make their sound or a glamorous movie star's real name?

These kinds of interests make you a natural for *how-to books*, which explain how something works or how to do something. *Trivia* books may also interest you. Some trivia books specialize in little-known facts about history or science. Others collect *mis*information—ideas that people used to believe in but that have since been proven wrong, or expert predictions that never worked out. If you enjoy finding out where the experts made their mistakes, you might look for one of those books. You might also want a book about movie or television trivia, or one about sports.

Sometimes discovering an offbeat fact can lead to a more serious interest. You might find, for example, that you want to go on to more in-depth reading about the *history of movies* in the United States, or find out *how a television station transmits* its program. A fascination with sports trivia could lead you to *biographies of sports figures*, such as Satchel Paige or Babe Ruth, or to a book about the *history of baseball,* or to adult or young adult *novels about sports.* Your teacher or librarian can help you find books that relate to the interests you already have.

► Are you one of those people who just likes thinking about people? Do you wonder why people act the way they do, or try to figure out what they really mean? Is analyzing someone's motives or predicting someone's behavior what you like to do best? Is it at least something that you'll spend an hour or two gossiping about with your friends?

If you're a "people person," then you've got plenty to read about. On the fiction side of the library, you would probably like just about anything, but *novels* are likely to interest you most. Both young adult and adult novels should hold your attention because what most novels are about is why people act the way they do and how they react to different situations. You'll have fun finding books about characters that seem to be like you and share similar problems. You might also want to read about people totally unlike you, who are interesting simply because they are so different.

On the nonfiction side of the library, start with *biographies*. These real-life stories of actual people often read like novels, telling the story of someone's life in fact rather than fiction. You might combine two interests by asking for a biography of someone who worked in a field that interests you. If you like politics, for example, you could read about the life of a U.S. president or about someone who spent years trying to win the right of women to vote. If you like science, you might read about Charles Drew or Marie Curie.

There are many kinds of nonfiction books about why people act as they do. *Psychology* books discuss and explain human behavior. *Anthropology* books talk about the ways people in different societies live their lives. *Travel* books can also be a way of finding out more about different people and how they act.

Exploring Books

If you have many book reports to write, you'll want to be on the lookout for books that interest you. However, even if you don't have an assignment hanging over your head, you may have fun exploring the kinds of books of interest to you. Browsing through a bookstore or a library can be a pleasant way to spend time. If you're not under pressure to buy something or check out a particular book, you might enjoy just looking around. Find the section of the library or the store that is likely to have the books you want.

Once you've found the section or sections that interest you, wander around. See what titles look interesting. "Preview" the books with interesting titles. Take them off the shelves, look them over, and maybe glance at a table of contents or index or dip into a paragraph or two. You might find a book that interests you, or one that you'll want to come back to later.

If you've already discovered a kind of book that you like, think about branching out. The more kinds of books you like, the more fun you'll have reading—and the easier time you'll have writing book reports.

14

Chapter 2:
Finding Your Way in the Library
(Check It Out)

Your teacher may assign you a book for a book report, or you may be expected to find your own book. Some teachers let you choose any book you want. Others let you choose, but expect you to get their approval on it before starting the report. Sometimes a teacher will expect you to find your own book on a particular topic, such as science or history.

In all of these cases, you'll have an easier time if you know how to use the library. Knowing how to use the library will also help you in doing research for your other school reports and in finding out about many other things that may interest you.

If you don't understand how a library is organized, you may be uneasy the first time you go in. All those books and magazines stacked in so many different places—how will you ever find the one you want? But once you understand the system, you'll be able to find your way straight to the information that you need. You might even find yourself picking up a little extra knowledge as you wander through the library!

Getting the Librarian to Help You

Whether you're going to your school library, your local library, or a huge city library, you'll find that they all have one thing in common: a librarian. The people who work in libraries are responsible for taking care of the books, magazines, and other possessions of the library. However, they also have another job—helping you. A librarian understands how to find books or information and is usually happy to help you, too.

So in many cases, especially when you are not looking for any one book in particular, a good first step in using the library is to talk to the librarian. The librarian can

► point out special book displays, such as books about a coming holiday, books about a current news event, or new books that the library just bought.

► explain how the library's fiction section is organized. Some libraries have special sections for mysteries, romances, westerns, and science fiction. Other libraries keep their paperbacks separated from the hardcover books.

► show you around the library's young adult or children's sections.

► point out other items that the library lends, such as records, cassettes, videotapes, and films.

► explain the library's rules, including how to get a library card, how to check out books, and how long you can keep books out.

► find a particular fact or explain where to look for it.

► provide ideas on types of books, authors, or sections of the library that might be of interest.

► demonstrate how to use the library's card catalog, Dewey decimal system, and reference books, so that you can find what you're looking for.

How to Find the Book You Want: Using the Card Catalog and the Dewey Decimal System

Most books in a library are numbered. They are filed on the shelves in numerical order, so you can always find a book if you know where to look. The *card catalog* is the place that tells you where to look.

The card catalog is a huge cabinet with lots of little drawers. Each drawer has letters on it, telling what part of the alphabet it covers (for example, *A–Ai* or *Sai–Sat*). Inside each drawer are cards that are filed in alphabetical order. Each card has information about one book.

Most nonfiction books have *three* cards in the card catalog: one that is filed according to the author's last name, one that is filed according to the title, and one that is filed according to the subject. Sometimes there will be even more cards for one book. For example, a book called *Knights and Dragons* by Molly Rogers would be listed under *K* for *Knights and Dragons*, the title; under *R* for Rogers, the author's last name; and under *M* for medieval history. However, it might also be listed under *F* for fairy tales, or *L* for legends, or even *W* for witchcraft, if it turns out that there are several chapters on dragons and witches.

No matter where the card is filed, it will always tell you the title of the book, the name of the author, the name of the publisher, the date of publication, and perhaps a little bit about the book's contents. The card will also give you a number that tells you where in the library you can find the book.

You can see how helpful a card catalog can be. Perhaps a friend or teacher has told you about *Knights and Dragons*, and you want to find that book for your report. You could just look in the card catalog under *K* for the title. Maybe you've read other books by Molly Rogers, such as *Castles and Kingdoms*, and you're wondering if she's written anything else that you might like. If you looked in the card catalog under *R* for the author, you could find out what other books by the same author were in the library.

Finally, you might be looking for all the books you can on a particular topic. You want to find a book about legends, or one about mythology, or one about medieval history. You would look in the card catalog under the name of one of those subjects. That way, you could find out all the books that a library had on that particular subject.

Most fiction books have only two cards in the card catalog—one listed by author and one listed by title. Fiction books usually aren't classified by subject.

Once you've found a card for the book you want, look in the upper left-hand corner of the card. The number in that corner will tell you where to find the book. Most libraries that you will use probably divide their books according to the *Dewey decimal system*, so this number is called the *Dewey decimal number*. The number is a kind of code. As you walk up and down in front of the library shelves, you will see that every book has a number and is put on the shelf in numerical order. If you know the number of your book, you can find it on the shelf.

Here is the basic Dewey decimal code. You don't have to memorize it, because all you really need to know is the number of the book you want. However, if you are browsing through the library, you can use this code to find the section of the library that is most likely to have the books that interest you. If you are looking for a good science book, stick around the 500s. For a biography, head on up to the 900s, and so forth.

Dewey Decimal System

000-099	General works (010—bibliographies; 030—encyclopedias; 080—collected works)
100-199	Philosophy (150—psychology)
200-299	Religion (220—Bible; 230—Christianity; 296—Judaism; 297—Islam; 299—Buddhism)
300-399	Social sciences (320—political science; 390—customs and folklore, anthropology)
400-499	Languages (423—dictionaries)
500-599	Science (510—math; 530—physics; 540—chemistry)
600-699	Applied science and technology (610—medicine; 620—engineering)
700-799	Fine arts and recreation (750—painting; 780—music; 790—recreation and sports)

800-899   Literature (811—poetry; 812—drama;
          820—English literature)
900-999   History, geography, biography
          (910—travel; 920—biography;
          950—Asian history)

As you can see, the Dewey decimal system has ten big categories and lots of other smaller categories. Some libraries have charts of the Dewey decimal system. If you are looking for a good book on, say, English literature, you could just go to the 820 section of the library and see what they had. The Dewey decimal numbers in that section would range from 820.0 up to 829.9, with each decimal point representing a smaller and smaller category, such as English literature written before 1600, or modern English literature. You could also ask the librarian for the general range of Dewey decimal numbers for the topic you are looking for.

In some libraries, fiction is located within a numerical system. In other libraries, fiction is kept separately. You find it on the shelves alphabetically, according to the author's last name. To find out where the fiction is in your library, ask the librarian—or look around yourself!

Some libraries use another system to catalog their books, known as the *Library of Congress system*. The Library of Congress uses both letters and numbers in its code. Just in case your library uses this system, here are the major categories of the Library of Congress system, along with some of the smaller categories.

Library of Congress System

A General works
  AC collections
  AE encyclopedias
  AZ general history

B Philosophy, psychology, religion
  BF psychology
  BR Christianity
  BM Judaism
  BP Islam
  BX special sects

C History: related studies
  CB civilization
  CT biography

D History (except the Americas)
  DA Great Britain
  DC France
  DK USSR
  DT Africa

E General history of America

F Local histories of North and South America

G Geography
  GC oceanography
  GN anthropology
  GT manners and customs
  GV sports, amusements, games

H Social sciences
  HB economics
  HE transportation
  HO family, marriage, home
  HT communities, race

J Political science

K Law

L Education

M Music

N Fine arts
  NA architecture
  ND painting
  NK industrial arts

P Language and literature
  PS American literature
  PZ fiction and children's literature

Q Science
  QA math
  QC physics

R Medicine
  RK dentistry
  RT nursing

S Agriculture
  SB plant culture
  SD forestry
  SF animal culture
  SK hunting sports

T Technology
  TA engineering
  TH buildings
  TR photography

U Military science

V Naval science

Z Bibliography and library science

For More Information: Reference Books and *The Readers' Guide to Periodical Literature*

Sometimes you will want to find out more about a topic that you have read about. The library has several different kinds of resources that may help you.

Reference books are books that include lists of facts or general overviews of a topic. You can *refer* to them to answer a question. The most well-known types of reference books are *dictionaries* and *encyclopedias*. To find out the meaning of a word, the date a book was written, or the birthplace of an author, you might look in a dictionary or encyclopedia.

Other types of reference books give specialized types of information. *Fact books* include books of lists, books of records, and so forth.

Biographical dictionaries list famous people in alphabetical order, giving basic information about who they are and what they did. One of the most famous dictionaries of this type is *Who's Who in America*.

Atlases are books of maps that often include other geographical information and statistics.

The Readers' Guide to Periodical Literature lists articles found in magazines and periodicals. Ask your librarian how to use this handy book.

Getting Help: Ask for What You Want

Now that you know what's in a library, you probably have a better idea of how to go about finding what you want. However, you may still want to get help from the librarian to point yourself in the right direction. Here are some ways that you might find yourself asking for help.

YOU: Excuse me, I'm looking for a couple of plays to read. I have to do a book report on a play.

LIBRARIAN: Any particular type of play? Musical comedy? Murder mystery?

YOU: I'm not really sure. We have to read some kind of play—I thought I'd just look around.

LIBRARIAN: You can find most of our plays under 812, over there with the rest of the 800s. Here is the Dewey decimal listing of different types of plays; that might give you a better idea of what we have. We also have plays for young people in our special young adult section.

YOU: Can you help me? I have to do a book report, and I'm not sure exactly what I want. But I thought something about space or space travel would be good.

LIBRARIAN: Our science fiction is over there. You might browse through it and see if anything appeals to you. There are also some science fiction books on the paperback racks. We don't catalog the paperback books, so you'll have to look through them yourself. I think there are some good science fiction novels among our paperbacks.

YOU: I'm not sure my teacher will let me do a report on science fiction.

LIBRARIAN: For nonfiction, you could check in the card catalog under *space, astronauts,* and maybe *rockets.* You might also look under some astronauts' names to see if we have any biographies, or you could just browse through the 600 section. Let me check and get you a more exact number, so you can go right to the books about space travel.

YOU: I'm giving an oral report about whales. I need to find out how many tons of food a whale eats every day.

LIBRARIAN: Have you checked the encyclopedia?

YOU: No, not yet.

LIBRARIAN: That's the first thing you should try. If that doesn't work, you might look in the card catalog under *whales.* That should point you to several books about whales. You could look in the books' indexes under *eating habits,* or *food*—that might save you a lot of time.

YOU: So I have to look at a lot of books?

LIBRARIAN: You might have to. You could also check some of the other reference books over there on that shelf. They give unusual or interesting facts, and they might tell you how much a whale eats. Look in the index under *whales.* If you don't find what you're looking for, come back and let me know. We'll try to think of something else.

Part II: WRITING YOUR REPORT

Chapter 3:
Getting Started
(First Things First)

One way to feel relaxed and confident about writing your report is to get yourself off to a good start. Make sure that you understand the assignment and that you've got all the information you need to begin your work.

Here are some questions you'll need the answers to before you start:

▶ *Have you gotten your teacher's permission to write a report on the book you've chosen?* Even if your teacher lets you choose your own book, you should make sure that he or she thinks that the book you've chosen will actually fulfill the assignment. If your teacher tells you to pick a book about history, and you pick a book about the history of ESP, that may be his or her idea of a history book—but it may not. The time to find out is before you've done any work.

▶ *How long is the report supposed to be?* If it's a written report, how many pages? If it's an oral report, how many minutes? Is there a maximum? Some teachers take off points if a report or paper is too long.

► *Should the report be single-spaced or double-spaced?* If your teacher doesn't care, you should double-space. It will make your report easier to read, and you'll have an easier time making it look neat. Again, though, check with your teacher. If Mr. Folio asks for a two-page report, he may mean two single-spaced pages. If you double-space your report, he may want you to write more pages.

► *Are you supposed to write on only one side of the paper?* It's usually a good idea to stick to one side—there's less to recopy if you make a mistake, and the final result will be easier to read.

► *Should the report be written in pencil? Pen? Typed? Any particular color?* Most teachers don't like you to use red because that's the color they use to correct. Green or purple ink can be hard to read. Usually, black or blue ink is best—unless your teacher has some other requirement. Some teachers, especially in high school, expect their students to submit typed papers.

► *When is the report due? Is there more than one deadline?* Some teachers want you to show them your work every step of the way—first your outline, then your rough draft, and finally your finished report. Other teachers just want the final copy. Whichever your teacher prefers, be sure you know when everything is due.

These things may seem like minor details, but to your teacher, who has to read 20 or 30 book reports, they may be important. In any case, some teachers

26

take off points for reports that are difficult to read or that don't follow the rules. Even if a teacher doesn't plan to penalize you, a messy report may affect your teacher's attitude as he or she reads it.

So your first step in writing a report should be to write down everything you need to know about the assignment. You should probably use a separate notebook or keep a separate file folder just for this book report. Write the assignment inside the notebook cover or on the front of the file folder so you won't lose it. What you write might look something like this:

BOOK REPORT DUE November 15th.
Ms. Filibuster's English class.
5 pages—double-spaced.
One side of page only!
Blue or black ink (green O.K., but no red!)

Outline due October 31st.
First draft due November 7th.
Final copy due November 15th.

Once you've made sure you understand the assignment, you should next make a schedule. Even if your teacher doesn't require you to hand in anything until your report is done, you will still find making a schedule a good idea. For one thing, it's a good way to make sure you will actually finish your report on time. If you're behind on your schedule, you'll know that you've got to put in more time on the report. For another thing, it's a good way to help yourself relax. If you're right on schedule—or even a little bit ahead—you can be pretty sure that you'll get everything done by the time it's due.

Making a schedule is also good practice. It helps you plan your time so that you're not putting off important work or worrying too much about upcoming deadlines.

To make a schedule, list each step that goes into writing your report. Your list might look something like this:

_____ Go to library.
_____ Choose my book.
_____ Get Mr. Folio's O.K.
_____ Read the book (take notes while reading).
_____ Make an outline.
_____ Write first draft.
_____ Revise first draft.
_____ Write final draft.
_____ Edit and proofread final draft. Retype or rewrite final draft if there are too many corrections on it.
_____ Turn in report.

Now fill in the last date first. You know when you have to turn in your report—that's part of the assignment. Then work backward. How long will it take you to edit and proofread your final draft? Let's say you want to allow two days for this step. In pencil, fill in the dates on which you plan to edit and proofread. Keep working backward. How long will it take you to write your final draft? Three days? Keep working backward until you get to the beginning of the schedule. If your beginning date is the same as the day you're making your schedule, you've timed everything very well!

If you've figured that in order to finish your report on time, you should have started a week ago, don't worry. Just go back over your schedule and allow yourself less time for each step. Be sure to keep to your schedule.

If you've figured that you don't need to start your report for another week or two, you might want to revise your schedule in the opposite direction, allowing more time for each step. That way, if you work as quickly as you've planned, you'll have the fun of finishing your work early, instead of taking the chance that you've shortchanged yourself. With practice, you'll learn how to schedule your work realistically.

Your final schedule might look something like this:

Oct. 29	Go to library.
Oct. 29	Choose my book.
Oct. 30	Get Mr. Folio's O.K.
Oct. 30-Nov. 3	Read the book (take notes while reading).
Nov. 4	Make an outline.
Nov. 4-6	Write first draft.
Nov. 7	DAY OFF. (It's always good to allow some time off after you finish a draft.)
Nov. 8-9	Revise first draft.
Nov. 9-11	Write final draft.
Nov. 12	DAY OFF. (This day off also gives you some "grace time" in case you are running late.)
Nov. 13-14	Edit and proofread final draft.
Nov. 15	Turn in report.

Chapter 4:
Reading Your Book
(Some Questions to Ask)

If you've chosen your own book, you are probably eager to read it. Even if your teacher has chosen the book, you can probably find something about it that interests you. *Starting with what interests you* is the first step in reading effectively for your book report.

After all, what is a book report? It is a report to other people about something you've read. When you've seen a movie that you hated or a good program on television, don't you report back to your friends about it? You say, "Don't go see that movie. It's boring!" or "Be sure to watch that new show on Wednesday nights—you'll really love it." Then you go on to tell your friends why the movie is boring ("I couldn't figure out what the mystery was about until just before the end. It was too confusing, so I got bored.") or why the show is great ("The actress is really beautiful and she's very funny, too. I was laughing all the time.").

Writing a book report works on the same principle. You are going to report to your reader what the book is about, how it made you feel, whether or not you liked it, and whether you'd recommend it to someone else. Therefore, it helps to have these questions in mind from the very beginning. If you *read in order to answer questions*, you'll be getting a real head start on your report. You'll be keeping in mind the questions your audience will have about your book and preparing the answers that your report will provide.

Of course, reading to answer questions does not mean that you look at a list of questions at the end of every page. It's more that you should keep some questions in the back of your mind—just as when you watch a movie, part of your mind may be thinking, "I wonder how my friends would like this? Oh, there's a part Bosley would like! He'd think that was funny. But Irene would hate this part—she doesn't like fights." Then, every so often, you may want to stop and think about the book you are reading. The following questions may help you with your thinking.

What is this book about? This may seem like a simple question, but it's actually a very important one. Being able to sum up in one or two sentences what a book is about is often rather difficult, but it's an important skill. You will probably want to begin your book report with a brief summary of the book. This lets your reader know what to expect and prepares him or her for the rest of your writing.

One way to think about this question is to imagine telling a good friend about your book. "I'm reading this great book," or "I'm reading a terrible book," you tell your friend. "It's about _____."

Telling what a book is about is more than just repeating the title or telling the story. It's summing up the main idea of the book. If you are reading a book about whales, for example, you wouldn't just tell your friend, "This book is about whales." Instead, you might say, "This book is about how

31

whales might die out if we don't do something to protect them," or "This book tells how whales live, going from the time they are born through their growing up and having babies of their own." The idea here is to describe the book in such a way that your friend couldn't confuse it with any other book. Of course, you won't worry about actually finding the words to answer this question while you are reading, but keep the question in the back of your mind.

What is the author's main point? What does the author want you to think by the time the book is over? Does he or she want you to think about what you can do to help save the whales? Is the main point that whales are beautiful animals and that we can enjoy watching them and learning about them? Imagining the author and what he or she is trying to say to you will help you to answer this question.

Even a fiction book has a main point. When people talk about "the moral of the story," they are talking about the idea the author wants you to believe by the end of the book. A novel about a young woman who has to decide whether to help some new friends cheat on their schoolwork, for example, might be making the following point: "At first, cheating may seem like a good idea, but the more you find out about it, the worse it seems." A story about a boy who feels lonely after his father dies may be saying, "Terrible things can happen in this life, but if you don't lose hope, you can find a way to go on and find new people to love."

While you are reading a book, you will focus most of your attention on following the story or understanding the facts. However, every so often, wonder where the author is leading you. By the end of the book, you should know what he or she is trying to make you think.

How does this book make you feel—and why? This two-part question is one of the keys to writing a good book report and to being a good reader. The more you feel while reading a book, the more you will enjoy the experience of reading. The more aware you are of *how* you feel and *why*, the better you will be able to share your feelings with others.

If you are reading a fiction book, is it making you laugh? Why? Maybe really wild, ridiculous, out-landish events happen, things that couldn't happen in real life but are fun to read about in a book. On the other hand, perhaps the main character keeps getting into trouble in ways that seem ordinary enough, but one thing keeps leading to another. Before you know it, things have gotten into a real tangle. Maybe you are laughing—or at least smiling—because you recognize the characters. They may seem like people you know. One of them may even remind you of yourself. Perhaps you are laughing because these characters are unlike any-body you know.

Maybe the book is making you sad. Perhaps you feel sorry for the characters, whose problems seem much bigger and more difficult than your own. On the other hand, maybe you see yourself in the characters, and you imagine how sad you would feel if you were going through what they are going through. Sometimes a book can remind you of things you are sad about in your own life. It may be a good kind of sadness, because you know from reading the book that other people have felt the same way as you. In other words, you're not alone in how you feel.

Sometimes a book can make you angry. If something unfair happens to one of the characters, you may get almost as angry as if it had happened to you.

Some books can frighten you. Ghost stories can be scary in a fun way, because you know that the events in the story never really happened. It may be scary to imagine *what if...*, but it's nice imagining it while you're safe all the time! On the other hand, a book might really scare you, reminding you of something in your own life that is a frightening problem. Again, this can be comforting, because you can see that you are not the only one to have the problem or to be frightened.

Even nonfiction books can make you feel happy or frightened, mad or sad. An inspiring biography can make you feel happy about what another human being was able to accomplish, sad about the problems that the person faced in life, and mad at the people who hurt the person you are reading about. A book that describes an earthquake might frighten you as you read about the disaster, then make you happy as you read about the bravery with which people faced it.

The more aware you are of your feelings, the more you will have to say about the book when it comes to writing your report. The more you know about *why* you feel the way you do, the better you will understand your book. Figuring out how a book works can be almost as much fun as actually reading the book!

Chapter 5:
Taking Notes
(Memory Jogging)

In Chapter 4, we talked about how to read actively by thinking about your feelings as you read. One way to help yourself think—and to remember what you thought—is to take notes. Taking notes also helps give you a head start in writing your report. You can look at your notes to help you remember how you felt while reading your book and to help you decide what you want to say.

There are two kinds of notes that will be helpful to you. One kind is the notes you take while you read. The other is the notes you jot down right after you finish your book. Both kinds will help you organize your thinking. The more organized your thinking, the easier it will be for you to write.

Taking Notes While You Read

The notes you take for a research report differ from the notes you take for a book report. You may already have learned that in a research report, you write down key facts and information that you can later use in your own writing.

For a book report, your job is not so much to use the book's information as to give other people an idea of what the book is about and how it made you feel.

35

While you read, have a pencil and paper handy. If something strikes your attention, jot down one or two words that will remind you of what you felt, plus the page number you were on when you got the idea. You don't have to spend a long time writing a detailed sentence. In fact, you probably shouldn't, because that will interfere with your reading. Nevertheless, you should make sure your note is clear enough for you to understand it later.

For example, if you are reading a novel and you find yourself laughing out loud at the scene where Jose loses control of the hose and sprays everybody at the garden party, you might write, "FUNNY—p. 28, Jose and hose at party." Later, when you have to explain why this book made you laugh, you'll have this note to remind you.

If you are reading a nonfiction book about dinosaurs and you are surprised to find out that they laid eggs, you could write, "Dinosaurs lay eggs!— p. 46." Reading the note will remind you of how interesting that fact was to you, helping you to explain what you liked about the book.

Taking notes can also help you to be more aware of your feelings as you read a book. It can help you think more clearly about what the author is trying to say and how that makes you feel. The more you feel and understand while reading a book, the more you will enjoy reading.

Taking Notes While Reading Fiction

Following are some kinds of notes you might find yourself taking while you read fiction.

The Plot's Main Events. If you are reading a book with a confusing or intricate story, you might want to jot down some of the twists and turns. Especially in a mystery story, the *plot*—the events that happen in the story—can be very important.

Your emotions are always the best clue to what to write down. If an event in the plot surprises you, jot it down. For example, if the heroine suddenly discovers that one of the suspects was in Hawaii the day the victim was murdered in New York, but also discovers a round-trip plane ticket in the suspect's coat, you might write, ''p. 72—Rd.-trip ticket, Haley maybe NOT in Hawaii?''

Likewise, if something very sad happens, you may want to note that. When the little boy's dog is hit by a car, and you find yourself feeling sad, you might write, ''Dog; accident; almost cried—p. 23.''

Turning Points. Have you ever read a book where you started out thinking one way about the story and somewhere along the way changed your mind? Maybe it's a murder mystery, and you switch from suspecting the mean old army colonel to wondering about the sweet little old lady who owns the bakery. Maybe you're reading a story about a family in which one of the sisters seems to be acting in a mean way. Halfway through, however, you decide that she is actually a nice person and it's the brother you don't like. Authors often like to play with their readers, surprising them or even tricking them in order to make a point.

These *turning points* are good places to note. For one thing, they often point the way to the moral of the story. The moral of the murder mystery we mentioned could be ''Appearances are deceiving. Sometimes 'nice' people are guilty and 'mean' ones are innocent." Noting the place where you started suspecting the "nice" character will help you understand how the author got the point across. The moral of the family story might be, "When we know the real reasons for someone's behavior, we may judge that person differently." You'll have an easier time understanding the author's point—and deciding whether or not you agree with it—if you understand how the author is shaping the story.

Can you think of what a note about a turning point might look like? For the murder mystery, you might write, "Maybe Miss Ellie guilty/Col. Ferr innocent?— p. 65," or you could note something more specific, such as "Why is Miss Ellie not at birthday party? *Suspicion!*—(p. 65)." Just be sure to give enough detail to help you remember what caused you to change your mind. After all, you could change your mind again!

For the family story, you might find yourself writing more about your emotions: "I liked Doug before, but now Janie seems nicer—p. 77," or "Why didn't Doug lend her the bike? Janie's feelings hurt—p. 77." These notes will help you remember both your reactions and the reasons for them.

This Makes Me Think of.... One good way to clue into your feelings while reading is to realize that the book is reminding you of something in your own life. Reading about two brothers having a fight might remind you of the time you told your brother to stay out of your room and how he responded by stealing your diary and hanging it on the cafeteria bulletin board. A story about a girl going on a trip with her father might remind you of a happy time you had with one of your parents—or it might make you think of a friend and a trip he took with his father.

Sometimes a book reminds you of another book, or of something you saw on television or at the movies. As you keep reading, you may find that your first impression was right—the heroine of your book is pretty much like the woman you saw on television. On the other hand, you may decide you were wrong. The two seemed similar at first glance, but it turns out that the woman in the book is much nicer and smarter than the woman on television, whereas the woman on television is a lot more brave and daring.

Whatever your impressions, jot them down! And if you find yourself changing your mind, jot that down, too. "Lisa = Alice," or "Pablo NOT like Jerry, too wimpy" are notes that will help you remember your reactions when you look them over later. You might also think about what the similarities mean. If a character reminds you of your sister, how does that help you understand what the author is saying? If the author is arguing that this character is unfortunate, whereas you think that your sister is the luckiest person in the world, does that mean that the author is wrong? Is there perhaps some other way that you might see your sister? Thinking about whether or not you agree with an author makes reading more interesting—and is a great way to learn more about your own life.

Good Jokes, High Points, Heart-Warming Moments, and Other Favorite Parts. When you are having a really great time reading, note that down. It can be as simple as "Margarita won the tournament, yea!— p. 55," or "Joe loves Lisa, school prom,—p. 98." You might put a star or an exclamation point beside the note to remind you that it stands for one of your favorite parts. It's also nice to know the page number of this part—you might want to go back and read it again!

Taking Notes While Reading Nonfiction

Following are some kinds of notes you might find yourself taking while you read nonfiction.

Author's Arguments. A very good question to ask yourself while reading nonfiction is, What does the author want you to do or think? Is she trying to teach you how to fix a chair? Is he trying to convince you to save the whales? Is she trying to get you to agree that astronomy is fascinating, or that space is mysterious, or that rocket travel is going to be very important by the year 2020? Most nonfiction books—especially the best ones—are more than just collections of facts. They're also *arguments* for or against something. A good author will try to convince you of his or her main point—even if that's only to convince you of how fascinating the topic is!

So every time you notice one of these arguments, jot it down: ''Whales in danger—p. 25''; ''They can be saved, but won't be easy—p. 30''; ''Whaling was O.K. in old days—p. 40''; ''Whaling bad now—p. 55''; and so on. As you can see, what you are jotting down is not *facts*, but *arguments*. That way, when it comes time to report on the book, you'll be able to talk about the author's main point—and to say whether or not it's something *you* agree with.

How would you jot down arguments in a book about astronomy, where the author isn't trying to get you to do something specific? Your notes on author's arguments might look something like this: "p. 4—astronomy important to ancient people/stars tell fortunes"; "p. 17—mystery of space—poetry!"; "p. 22—astronomy key to space travel—riches, minerals"; "p. 40—fun to find new stars"; and so forth. As you can see, these "arguments" aren't as direct as those in the book about saving the whales, but they can help you remember why the author is writing the book and what he or she thinks is important. Once again, noting the arguments can help you decide whether or not you agree with the author. Perhaps you don't think it's "poetic" to ponder the mysteries of space. Maybe you think looking for new stars sounds boring, not fun, the way the author seems to think. Your opinion is important, but you can't have an opinion until you know what you're having an opinion about.

Fun Facts. Sometimes reading a nonfiction book can make you laugh, or feel surprised, or stop a minute and think. Hearing how far apart the stars are, how much a dinosaur egg weighs, how tall the pyramids are, or how the Aztecs used to tell time can intrigue or delight you. So note those moments down. You can put down either the whole fact— "p. 56—Cheops pyramid, 138 meters"—or just a reminder—"Dinosaur eggs, HEAVY!—p. 25." In either case, be sure you've noted the page number so that you can check back to confirm your accuracy. You might want to use one or two of these facts to demonstrate how interesting the book was—or just to impress your friends.

Sad or Scary Facts. Again, your own emotions are the best clue to what you should write down. If reading about endangered whales or cruel kings makes you sad, frightened, or angry, that's a good sign that you've hit on an important point of the book. In any case, you've hit on an important part of your reaction to it. Any time you feel strongly while reading, note it down. These notes will be useful to you when you are trying to describe the book and your opinion of it in your report.

These notes might or might not have page numbers, depending on whether you are reacting to one specific fact or to several pages of reading: "Light from star takes seven years to reach us—scary long distance"; "Why whalers continue? Unfair!"

This Makes Me Think of.…Something you read in a nonfiction book could remind you of something in your own life or the life of a friend, or it might remind you of another book, a movie, a television show, a story you heard once, or another "fun fact." Jotting down your associations with a book can be an interesting way of understanding a book's message more deeply. If part of the reason you enjoyed reading about astronomy was that it reminded you of *Star Trek*, what does that tell you about who else might enjoy the book?

Taking Notes After You Finish Reading

After you have finished reading a book, take a moment to enjoy the feeling. Smile as you think of how happy the hero and heroine will be together, or as you remember how Max and Maxine won the track meet for Maxwell High. Then take advantage of the fact that the book, its events, and your feelings about it are all fresh in your mind. Quickly jot down the answers to the following questions:

1. What is the main idea of this book?

For fiction: What is the moral of the story?

For nonfiction: What does the author want you to do or to think?

2. What are the book's main points?

For fiction: What are the main events in the plot?

For nonfiction: What are three or four of the author's main arguments?

3. What are some examples of interesting items in the book?

For fiction: What are some incidents that made you feel strongly? Your favorite or least favorite parts? People you loved or hated? Times you felt especially happy, angry, sad, or scared?

For nonfiction: What are some fun or scary or upsetting facts from the book?

4. Overall, how did this book make you feel?

5. Was there anyone that this book strongly reminded you of? Who?

6. Who do you think should read this book? Who should not read this book?

These six questions give you a good working outline from which to write your report. However, now is not the time to think about outlines. We'll talk more about how to write outlines in Chapter 6. For the moment just after you finish a book, what you should be most concerned with is your immediate impressions. Jotting down answers to these questions off the top of your head is often a valuable way of getting your strongest, most useful reactions.

Chapter 6:
Making an Outline
(Order in the Report)

Writing an outline helps you organize your thoughts. That way, while you are writing, you can focus on saying what you want to say, without having to worry about what comes next. You'll know what comes next: Just look at your outline.

Most of the outlines you will write will be for your eyes only. You just need to make sure that you can follow the information easily enough that it won't interfere with your writing process. However, sometimes it's useful to show your outline to your teacher. That way, he or she can give you advice or make suggestions about topics you may want to add before you start writing. Some teachers require an outline to be turned in as an early part of the assignment, so they can make sure you're on the right track before you've done too much work.

If you're writing an outline for yourself alone, don't worry about how you phrase things. Forget about spelling, grammar, and punctuation. Just put down some key words that will remind you what you want to say.

If you're writing an outline for a teacher or for someone else, you'll want to take more care with your writing. (You might want to write a rough draft outline to get your thoughts in order, then recopy it neatly, making any necessary corrections.) In this case, think of your outline as giving the other person directions. If your teacher or some other person had to write your paper, could he or she do so based on your outline? Thinking this way will help to keep your writing clear.

What Should Your Outline Include?

In Chapter 5, we suggested some basic questions that you can use to organize your book report. Here are those questions again, this time in outline form.

Outline for Fiction Book Report

I. Main information
   A. Book's title
   B. Book's author
   C. Other information required by teacher (publisher, date of publication, and so forth)
   D. Main idea—what is the moral of the story?

II. Main Events in the Story
   A. One turning point
   B. A second turning point
   C. The most important scene in the story

III. Interesting Incidents
   A. How did the book make you feel? Did it remind you of anyone or anything?

B. Example of incident that made you feel that way
C. Example of another incident that made you feel that way

IV. Evaluation
    A. What did you like about the book?
    B. What did you not like about the book?
    C. Who should read this book?
    D. Who would not enjoy this book?

As you can see, this outline incorporates a lot of the questions we've suggested you think about while you read the book and while you take notes. For more about how to organize your notes and your thinking into outline form, see page 47.

Outline For Nonfiction Book Report

I. Main Information
    A. Book's title
    B. Book's author
    C. Other information required by teacher (publisher, date of publication, and so forth)
    D. Main idea—what does the author want you to do or think?

II. Author's Main Arguments
    A. One major argument
    B. Another major argument
    C. The author's most important argument

III. Interesting Facts
    A. How did the book make you feel?
    B. Example of fact that made you feel that way
    C. Example of another fact that made you feel that way

IV. Evaluation
    A. What did you like about the book?
    B. What did you not like about the book?
    C. Who should read this book?
    D. Who would not enjoy this book?

Of course, you may want to make some changes in either of these outlines, based on your actual book. Nevertheless, you can use these as models to help you get started on your own outline.

How to Organize Your Notes

Start with the basic outline. Copy one of the models in this book, or write your own outline. In either case, be sure to leave plenty of room between each capital letter, so that you will have space to add more notes if you need to. You might want to do this work in pencil, so that you can erase if you change your mind.

Now, with the outline in front of you, look over all your notes, both the ones you made while reading your book and the ones you made right after. Take a different color pen from the one you wrote your notes in. Cross out any notes that seem dull, repetitive, or misguided. Maybe you wrote the same note several times, remarking over and over again how much you liked the heroine of the story. That's good information—it shows you felt strongly—but you don't really need to see the same note in five different places. Cross out all but one of the notes. Maybe at one point you thought the author was telling you that whaling in the nineteenth century was a good thing, but as you read on, you realized that she actually meant just the opposite. Cross out the note that seems wrong, leaving only the one that seems right now that you have finished. You might want to put a star or a check mark beside any notes that seem especially important.

Now it's time to divide your notes into categories. Write them in under the categories of the outline where they seem to belong. At this point, don't worry about the order you put them in. Just divide them up.

Sample Fiction Outline—Notes Partly Organized

I. Main Information
    A. *Jane Eyre*
    B. Charlotte Bronte
    C. Classic Publishing Company, 1982
    D. It's important to stand by what you believe in, even if sometimes you'd rather give in.

II. Main Events in the Story
    A. Jane goes away to school.
    B. Jane gets into a fight with her family.
    C. Jane meets Mr. Rochester.
    D. Jane runs away from Mr. Rochester.
    E. Jane becomes a governess.

NOTE: Because you are still organizing your notes, you may not have decided which is the most important scene in the story. Don't worry. For now, just write down all the "main events" that were in your notes or that you remember now. You'll finish organizing them later.

III. Interesting Incidents
    A. The book made me feel sad most of the time—ending was happy.
    B. Happy—Jane finds a friend at school.
    C. Sad—Jane is lonely, fights with family.
    D. Happy—Jane and Rochester get married.
    E. Sad—Jane has to leave Rochester.

IV. Evaluation
    A. Liked—reading about Jane because she was strong and knew what she wanted. I really wanted her to win. Hoped she would be happy.
    B. Not liked—nothing. (It was sad a lot of the time. Jane was sad—made me sad. But then happy ending.)
    C. Everybody should read this book.
    D. I don't know who would not enjoy it.

As you can see, some of the notes come from reading. Others fit right into the outline because you used the questions in Chapter 5 as your model. This outline is still in rough form, but it's a good start.

Sample Nonfiction Outline—Notes Partly Organized

I. Main Information
    A. *Siberia*
    B. Francis Johnson
    C. Falcon Books, 1970
    D. Siberia is an interesting place that most people don't understand. It's not the way you think it is.

II. Author's Main Arguments
    A. Siberian people are very friendly.
    B. He expected Siberia to be all bad, but it wasn't.
    C. People should learn more about Siberia.

III. Interesting Facts
    A. The book made me interested to learn about this foreign people.
    B. Temperatures go down to 40° below zero and even colder.
    C. Eskimolike people eat reindeer steaks.
    D. Engineers have to figure out how to build when the ground is frozen.

IV. Evaluation
    A. Liked—reading about the engineers and finding out about the Eskimos (native people).
    B. Didn't like—some parts go on too long; lots of numbers and statistics, boring!

C. People who like to find out about foreign countries would like this.

D. People who don't like numbers would not enjoy this.

Now that you've got all your notes organized into an outline, go over your work, Roman numeral by Roman numeral. First, ask yourself, *Do I have too many items under each Roman numeral?* In the fiction outline, for example, five main events are listed under Roman numeral II. This may be too many. If you really described each event, you might take up your whole book report just describing what happens. Go over a section that seems too long, and just cross out anything that seems less interesting or important.

Next, ask yourself, *Is my information in the right order?* Sometimes when you are organizing notes, you will just naturally put them into a clear and interesting order, but sometimes you have to play with them a little. Here are some things to keep in mind while putting your notes in order:

► *Does the reader need to know one thing in order to understand something else?* Make sure you don't put the cart before the horse. In fiction, we need to know that two characters are friends before we can understand why it's important when they have a fight. In nonfiction, we need to know that the whales are in danger before we know how the author thinks they can be saved.

► *Do you want your facts to come in chronological order?* "Chronological order" means the order in which they happened *in time*. If you are reporting on a history book, you might want your "interesting facts" to be organized with the earliest information first, working your way up from slavery through the Civil War up to Reconstruction. If you are reporting on a fiction book, you might want your "interesting incidents" to be organized in the same order that they happen in the story. Chronological order has the advantage of usually being clear to the reader, but keep in mind that there are other ways to organize your facts.

▶ *Are you comparing and contrasting different facts or feelings?* Sometimes you want to talk about two contrasting facts or feelings. In that case, it's often helpful to your reader if you put all of one kind of fact together, then all of another. If the author of the book on whales thinks some kinds of whaling are good while other kinds are bad, for example, you might want to talk about all the good kinds, then about all the bad kinds, instead of going back and forth. In the fiction outline under Roman numeral III, the writer has gone back and forth between happy and sad incidents. It might make sense to put all the happy incidents together and all the sad ones together.

▶ *Do you want to move from the least important point to the most important point, or do you want to start with the main idea and then give the secondary ideas?* Either of these orders may help you build an argument. In the nonfiction outline under Roman numeral II, the writer has moved from the least important argument—Siberian people are very friendly—to the most important argument—People should learn more about Siberia. The writer might have put the same items in the opposite order:

A. People should learn more about Siberia.
B. He expected Siberia to be all bad, but it wasn't.
C. Siberian people are very friendly.

Sometimes you need to start with your main argument, so that people can understand the secondary arguments. Other times, working up to your main argument is better: You hold the reader's interest because each piece of information appears more important than the one that came before. The reader wants to keep reading because he or she knows that something good is coming. You have to decide which way will work best for your report.

Once you have thought about what order your material should go in, cross letters out or use arrows to rearrange your notes. Then copy your outline neatly so that you can use it to write. While you are copying, think again about what you have included under each category. Have you left anything out? Have you put too much in? Is your information in the best possible order to hold your reader's interest and make your points clear?

Of course, you will always have a chance to change your mind as you write. You've still got a rough draft and a final draft to go. You can always play around with your ideas then. Nevertheless, the more work you do on your outline, the less you'll have to do later. The more thinking you do ahead of time, the more free your mind will be while you write, so that you can concentrate on choosing words rather than on organizing ideas.

Once you've made a final outline, pick up a pencil. Write the number of pages your report is supposed to be at the top of the outline. Then go through each Roman numeral and write in pencil how long you think it should be when you write your report. Look through all your pencil marks. Does everything add up to the right number of pages? You may need to erase and rewrite some figures, so that your report is neither too long nor too short. Again, you don't have to stick to these lengths very strictly—they're just to give you an idea. However, if you've put down that section II should be one paragraph and it runs into two pages, you know something is wrong.

Following are two samples of what your final outlines might look like.

Sample Fiction Outline—Organized   5 pages

I.   Main information (1 paragraph)   ½ page
  A. *Jane Eyre*
  B. Charlotte Bronte
  C. Classic Publishing Company, 1982
  D. It's important to stand by what you believe in, even if sometimes you'd rather give in.

II. Main Events in the Story   1½ pages
  A. Jane gets into a fight with her family.

B. Jane goes away to school.
C. Jane meets Rochester and falls in love.
D. Jane runs away.
E. Jane and Rochester get married.

Turn to page 48, and compare this outline with the partly organized one. Do you see how the writer has taken out some items and added others? She has also put the events in the story into chronological order. That will make it easier for the reader to follow the main events.

III. Interesting Incidents   2 pages
    A. This book made me feel sad most of the time, but the ending was happy.
    B. Sad—Jane is lonely, fights with family.
    C. Sad—Jane has to leave Rochester.
    D. Happy—When Jane is at school, finds friend.
    E. Happy—Jane had to leave Rochester but then comes back and gets married.

Look back at page 48, and see how the author has revised the earlier outline. She has put all the happy parts together and all the sad parts together. She has put the happy parts in the order they happened in the book, and done the same with the sad parts. Remember that this is just one way to organize your notes—think about the way that will work best for you.

IV. Evaluation   1 page

    A. Liked reading about Jane because she was strong and knew what she wanted. I wanted her to be happy and get what she wanted.

    B. Not liked—nothing. A lot of the book was very sad. (Jane had sad life.) Then happy ending, so O.K.

    C. Everybody should read this book.

    D. I don't know who would not enjoy it.

Sample Nonfiction Outline—*Organized*   **2 pages**

I.   Main information (1 paragraph)   ½ page

    A. *Siberia*

    B. Francis Johnson

    C. Falcon Books, 1970

    D. Siberia is an interesting place that most people don't understand. It's not the way you think it is.

II.   Author's Main Arguments   ½ page

    A. Siberian people are very friendly.

    B. He expected Siberia to be all bad, but it wasn't.

    C. People should learn more about Siberia.

III.   Interesting Facts   ½ page

    A. This book made me interested to learn about this foreign people.

    B. Eskimolike people eat reindeer steaks.

    C. Temperatures go down to 40° below zero and even colder.

D. Engineers have to figure out how to build when the ground is frozen.

Notice how the writer changed the order of the items in this section. Now the two items about people are together—A and B—and the two items about temperature are together—C and D. It makes sense to put C before D, because we need to know how cold it gets before we know that the cold is a problem for engineers.

IV. Evaluation   ½ page
    A. Liked reading about the engineers and finding out about the Eskimos (native people).
    B. Didn't like some parts that went on too long. Lots of numbers and statistics—boring.
    C. People who like to find out about foreign countries should read this.
    D. People who don't like numbers should not.

Notice that since the nonfiction report was supposed to be only two pages long, the writer has divided the report into four equal parts, half a page each. However, when it actually comes to writing the report, it might turn out that section I will be shorter and section III will take up more space. That would probably make the report more interesting, because section III is more interesting than section I and should get a bigger share of the paper. The writer should keep this in mind while revising the first draft. For now, however, the outlines are done, and it's time to start writing.

Chapter 7:
Writing Your Report
(Putting It All Together)

Because you've done so much thinking and planning ahead of time, writing your report should be a lot easier than if you had just sat down to start writing right after you read your book. You already know what each paragraph should be about. Now you're ready to begin writing.

Even the writing process can be broken down into steps: 1) rough draft; 2) revision; 3) final draft; and 4) editing and proofreading.

Everyone gets nervous when starting to write—even professional writers. Breaking the writing process down into several steps helps you to feel less nervous. It allows you to concentrate on one thing at a time. Writing your paper step by step gives you the freedom to say clearly what you want to say.

Of course, writing is a very personal process. You may be one of those lucky people who can write a report the first time and have it turn out perfectly. If so, use your instincts and write the best report you can. Enjoy your ability to write quickly and easily. However, if you feel anxious about starting your report, don't worry. Almost everybody feels that way. You can learn to work through those feelings by counting on the writing process.

Writing a Rough Draft

Writing a rough draft means that you don't have to worry about spelling, grammar, or punctuation. You write a sentence knowing that you didn't say exactly what you meant, but that you'll have a chance to go back and fix it later. The important thing about a rough draft is to try not to worry about what you're writing. If something gives you trouble, leave it alone (maybe putting a mark in the margin to remind you what the problem is), and come back to it later. You might see the solution to your problem more easily then—or you might see that there really wasn't any problem at all and your writing was better than you thought!

If you're one of those people who has to think hard about each sentence, don't worry. There are no points given for speed in writing a rough draft. Just try not to get hung up on any one sentence or word. Give yourself permission to take it easy by promising yourself that you can be hard on yourself later, if you want.

Some teachers may ask to see your rough draft, just to be sure that you are following every step of the writing process. However, if they are really interested in a *rough draft*, they will understand that you may have made mistakes in grammar, sentence structure, or other parts of writing. Not worrying about mistakes is what a rough draft is for. That's what gives you the freedom to explore your ideas.

Picture Your Audience

Start your writing by imagining your audience. It helps to picture someone you feel comfortable with, someone you would enjoy talking to—someone who will just love your report. With whom would you like to discuss your book? Your best friend? Another sports fan? A science fiction fan who's never heard of this particular book? Look over your outline, and imagine telling the person you've pictured about this book so that he or she will understand what the book's main idea is, what the main events or arguments are, why you liked or didn't like it, and whether he or she will like it.

Now you can begin to write.

Use Your Outline—But Change It, Too

Your outline is there as a guide for you. It means you can concentrate on every paragraph, knowing that you don't have to worry about what to say next because the next paragraph is already described in your outline.

However, one of the interesting things about writing is what you find out while doing it. Maybe the order of ideas that seemed so good while you were writing the outline now seems boring or confusing. Maybe as you are actually forming the sentences, you realize that without explaining what a skating contest is, one of the turning points that you're describing won't make sense. Maybe you remember some fact or incident that's even more interesting than the ones in your outline, or that fits in better with the rest of what you're writing.

If you get a good idea that differs from your outline, go with it. You've always got the outline to go back to if your new idea doesn't work out. That's what a rough draft is for: to play with, to experiment with. Let your outline be a guide, but remember—you wrote it. You can change it.

Revising Your Report

It's always a good idea to take a day off after you've finished writing a draft. (Remember the schedule on page 29?) Taking a day off allows you to come back to your work with a fresh eye. You can really look at what you've said as though somebody else had written it, catching all the places that are confusing or not quite right. Even if you haven't left yourself time for a day off, try to take a good break between writing and revising. Go get yourself a snack, listen to a record, or even watch a little television (as long as you don't get so involved in your "break" that you don't feel like coming back to work!). Do something that has nothing to do with writing, and try to "forget" what you said in your report.

Then, when you do go back to your report, try to read the whole thing through aloud, without stopping. As you read, use a different color pen or pencil from the one you wrote in to make marks in the margin. Put a little check or dash beside every place that you think needs work. It might help to write a little note like "confusing" or "Jane NOT rich"—something to remind yourself of what the problem is. However, don't write anything that will distract your attention from your reading. The idea is to get an overall view of what you have written and to imagine how it would sound to another person.

It helps to pretend that your imaginary audience

is in the room with you, listening to you read. What will this person understand? What will this person be confused by? How will that sentence sound to him or her? Have you said exactly what you meant? Have you written a sentence too short to make sense or too long to be easily understood? Trying to see your report through the eyes of another person and to hear it through another person's ears can help you see what you want to change.

People have different reactions to their rough drafts. Some writers get very discouraged. They hate everything they've written. They're sure that they can't write well at all, that they should just give up now before making any more of a fool of themselves. They see only their mistakes.

Other writers love their rough drafts. They are amazed at what good writers they are, after all. They can't believe they've chosen each word so well—and in a rough draft, too! Except for a period here and a comma there, these writers think their work is perfect.

Both of these reactions have one thing in common: They're a way of avoiding having to do any more work! If your writing is so terrible, why bother fixing it? If your writing is already perfect, you don't have to fix it. However, the truth is probably somewhere in between for both kinds of writers. Very few writers can come up with a perfect rough draft. That's why even professional writers have *editors*, people to help them see where they could make their writing better. At the same time, no writer is hopeless. The whole reason for a first draft is to get your ideas onto paper, not to beat yourself up for failing to write a perfect report on your first try. Now that your ideas are out there, you've got the chance to play with your writing to make it better.

If you're one of the those people who loves every word of a first draft, enjoy it! It's wonderful to feel that you've done a good job. However, give yourself the chance, perhaps after a longer break, to go back and make absolutely sure that you've said everything you want to say exactly the way you want to say it. Most writers rewrite their drafts once, twice, or three times. Some writers even do ten or twenty revisions! You don't have to go this far for a simple book report, but remember that there's very little writing that can't be improved by another going-over.

If you're someone who hates everything in the first draft and wants to give up on writing, calm down. You just need to understand that this negative feeling is your way of reacting to the writing process. However, that doesn't mean you have to quit. You may need to take a longer break, in order to give yourself time to recover, or you may need to just start focusing on the task at hand, figuring out exactly what needs to be fixed in your report. Sometimes revising a whole piece of writing can seem overwhelming, but fixing one detail at a time seems much easier. Breaking down your work—so that you're only worried about one problem at a time— can help you break through your negative feelings. In any case, don't despair. Many good writers *feel* their work is bad at first, but that doesn't mean it *is*. Remember, a rough draft is supposed to be rough.

Following are some common problems to watch out for while revising your rough draft.

Organization

Even though you followed your outline, somehow your report seems a little confusing. The ideas don't seem to fit together the way you thought, or you've found that some information that is needed to make the report make sense is somehow missing.

Try "talking through" a place that isn't making sense to you. Picture your audience, and then tell the person, one sentence at a time, what you're trying to say. Then try it again, this time writing down the sentences. That can help straighten out difficulties.

Length

Your report is too short—or maybe too long. Perhaps some paragraphs or sections go on longer than what you had figured in the outline. You've got one or two sentences about why you liked the book, with almost two pages on what happens in it. The balance feels wrong to you.

It's usually easier to cut than to add, so start with that. Figure out how many lines or sentences you would have to cut to make your report, or the paragraph in question, the right length. Then—in pencil, so you can change your mind later—draw a line through them. Reread your work, aloud if possible, without the crossed-out sentences. If you're having too much trouble picturing the report without them, you may need to make another rough copy of this part of your work so that you can really see what happens without the extra sentences. Does your paragraph still make sense? Maybe you still need to add a word or two, or another phrase—but you were still able to cut several sentences.

If you're really frustrated with this process, you might want to start over on this part of the report. Tell yourself that you are allowed only five lines or three sentences. Then ask yourself what your audience absolutely needs to hear within those limits. Remember, this kind of rewriting and rethinking *is* the writing process. It's the reason you wrote a rough draft, and the reason you've allowed time to revise it.

If all or part of your report is too short, go back to your outline and your notes. What else might you include that you left out the first time? Often this is enough to solve your problem. If you feel you've already used everything in your notes, look again at the questions on page 43. Ask yourself these questions again, and let your imagination run wild. That should spark some new ideas.

Fragments and Run-ons

Remember that a sentence should express a complete thought. A fragment is only part of a sentence. If you find fragments in your rough draft, combine them with other sentences or turn them into complete thoughts.

A run-on combines two or more sentences without proper punctuation to separate the thoughts. A run-on can usually be corrected with a period or semicolon.

In revising your report, you may also come across a sentence that goes on and on when it should be broken down into separate thoughts. If you find sentences in your paper that are really several thoughts strung together with "and" or "but," decide how to break them up.

Reading your work aloud is an excellent way to catch fragments and run-ons. When reading, you naturally want to take pauses or breaths. You can let your natural rhythm be a guide for the length of your sentences.

Paragraphs

Each paragraph is supposed to cover one main idea, so that all the sentences in that paragraph concern the same idea. If you have paragraphs running for an entire page, or if you have started new paragraphs every two sentences, you might want to think about reparagraphing. Some paragraphs *are* meant to be very long or very short, but be absolutely sure that you have intended this style if that is what you choose. Think of paragraphs as the place where the reader takes a longer breath or pause before going on to the next idea.

Checklist for Revisions

Of course, you should also keep spelling, capitalization, and punctuation rules in the back of your mind as you revise your rough draft, but you don't need to worry about them too much at this stage. They will be a greater concern for you at the editing and proofreading stage.

What you should do, however, is try to make each sentence clear and correct according to the rules of Standard English. Think about other grammatical points: avoiding double negatives, making sure pronouns refer clearly to their antecedents, and having subjects and verbs agree. You may want to go through your work once for the bigger writing problems, then a second or third time to work on grammar, and then take a quick look at spelling, capitalization, and punctuation. Be sure you have your ideas in order—saying exactly what you want to say—before you go on to worry about grammar and spelling. The following checklist might help you remember what to look for.

_____ Organization
       _____ ideas in right order
       _____ no important ideas left out
       _____ no unimportant ideas left in
       _____ sentences say what I mean
_____ Length
       _____ each paragraph or section is right length
       _____ whole report is right length
_____ No fragments
_____ No run-ons
_____ Paragraphs not too long or too short and express ideas clearly
_____ Grammar
       _____ no double negatives
       _____ pronouns clearly refer to antecedents
       _____ pronouns agree with antecedents
       _____ subjects and verbs agree
_____ Quick checks
       _____ spelling
       _____ capitalization
       _____ punctuation

Your revision process is finished. If possible, take another break. Then go on to write your final draft.

Writing Your Final Draft

Writing your final draft will be a lot easier than writing your rough draft. You've already got a revised rough draft to work with. The major thinking and figuring-out part of your report is finished. Now you should just be concerned with getting an idea of how each sentence looks and sounds.

Begin by copying over your revised rough draft neatly onto another piece of paper. If you notice any spelling or grammatical errors while copying, change them. If you see a way to make a sentence better, now is your chance to do it. Be careful, however. Sometimes a little change in one sentence doesn't fit in with what comes in the next sentence. Read through the rest of your paragraph before making any writing changes.

At this point, your work should be nearly done. However, it's these last few finishing touches that can help make the difference between a good report and a very good report. Again, read your report all the way through aloud. Listen to each sentence as though you were someone else—the audience you have imagined.

If possible, find a real audience to read your report to! A parent, brother, sister, or friend can tell you if something is boring, doesn't make sense, or is hard to understand. That gives you a chance to change it before your teacher sees it. However, remember that this is *your* report. If you don't agree with your audience, stand by your work. Consider the criticism, but let the final decision on whether or not to take it be your own. After all, your name will be on it.

After you have finished your final draft, read through it one or two more times, silently or aloud. Make any changes you want—but beware of the tendency to keep changing back and forth on little details. Sometimes nervous writers give too much importance to tiny problems, just because they want their work to be perfect. Try to remember that even the best writers in the world usually don't write perfect papers—but they can write very good papers, and so can you.

When you've finished writing the final draft of your work, leave it for a while. If possible, take a day off, as we suggested on the schedule on page 29. At least give yourself a break before going on to the next page.

Editing and Proofreading Your Report

Now is the time to catch all the tiny little problems that you've been putting off. Earlier, you were concerned with your ideas; then you worried about your writing, your sentences, and your grammar. Now you can give your attention to all the picky little things that don't affect the content of your paper, but do affect how your reader reacts to it.

If you don't like being careful about small details at this stage of the process, stop and think about your reader for a moment. A messy paper or one that does not give the necessary information (such as the title of the book, the name of the author, and your name) takes more time to read and is less pleasant to spend time with. A misspelled word can cause a reader to have to stop and think about which word you meant, or just to notice that the word looks different. This kind of interruption annoys the reader and takes attention away from what you are trying to say.

Your main purpose in writing the report has not been to please your teacher, but to figure out how you felt about the book and then to communicate those feelings through writing. Still, now that you've done that, take a moment to make things a little easier on the reader. The extra care you take now with your book report may result in a better grade later.

Checklist for Editing and Proofreading Final Draft

_____ Format: Have you followed your teacher's rules about
      _____ where the book's title should be
      _____ where the author's name should be
      _____ where your name should be
      _____ whether to include other information, such as your room number, your teacher's name, the name of the class, the date, and so forth?

_____ Neatness
      _____ handwriting readable
      _____ followed instructions about single-spacing or double-spacing
      _____ followed instructions about color of ink
      _____ wrote on only one side of the page

_____ Spelling (use a dictionary for any word you're unsure of)

_____ Capitalization

_____ Punctuation

_____ Last-minute grammar check
      _____ no double negatives
      _____ pronouns clearly refer to antecedents
      _____ pronouns agree with antecedents
      _____ subjects and verbs agree

If you need to recopy your report after making these last-minute changes, do so. The extra time will be worth it, because a neat report will be much better received by your teacher. If you can fix up your report without writing it over, so much the better. In either case, resist the temptation to make lots of changes in the writing itself. At this stage, it's likely that these changes only come out of nervousness. You've already done a lot of good work—now try to relax and enjoy it!

Chapter 8:
Unusual Ideas for Reports
(Creative Creating)

Most of this book has been concerned with how to write a basic book report. However, if your teacher is interested in reports with more depth or in unusual ideas for a book report, you may want to consider some other formats. You might also learn more about your feelings for a book by choosing different ways of writing about it.

Go into More Depth

If your teacher wants longer or more in-depth book reports, you should be able to start with the ideas we've already discussed. However, you could write an outline that would incorporate more detail, going further into your reasons for feeling the way you do and allowing you to think more deeply about why the book made you feel that way.

One way to add more depth to your reports is to add the following question to every point on your outline: *How did the author make this happen?* If you have said the book made you laugh, you may already have explained that you found the long, involved series of accidents funny or that you were laughing at a ridiculous character. Now take it a step further. What was funny about the long string of accidents? You might write something like this:

I enjoyed *Zany Times at Douglass High* because it made me laugh. The characters were always getting into messy situations that kept getting worse and worse. [Now for more explanations: *How did the author make this happen?*] Characters would start out in a situation that seemed easy enough. For example, in Chapter 1, Buddy has to buy a birthday cake for his father's party. However, at each step of the way, something happens to trip him up. The harder he tries to fix things up, the worse everything gets.

Notice how the writer of the above paragraph uses an example to make his point. The writer explains *how* he felt (he enjoyed the book); *why* he felt that way (the book made him laugh); and *what* it was about the book that made that true (the characters kept getting into messy situations). Then he goes on to give more detail about how the book worked, the mechanics of why it was funny.

If the writer then wanted to say that the book was also funny because of its ridiculous characters, he might write something like this:

Another funny thing about *Zany Times* was its crazy characters. They really made me laugh. They were always doing things that you'd never expect anybody to do, but somehow it was funny. For example, Mr. Pickles, the shop teacher, kept repeating the same thing, "Everybody should know how to use a saw." Because he keeps repeating it, you keep expecting him to say it. However, when Freddy gets stuck in the doorway and they have to saw through the door frame to get him out, it's very funny to read Mr. Pickles saying this again. For once, this "stupid" saying actually makes sense!

Notice how the writer followed the same format in the above paragraph: (1) how he felt (like laughing); (2) why he felt that way (the book was funny); (3) what was so funny (the crazy characters); and (4) more detail about *why* the characters were funny. Sometimes you can leave out the first point—how you felt—if you've already explained this in an earlier paragraph and this paragraph is just giving more reasons for the same feeling.

Notice also how the writer uses examples to explain what he means. The writer does not just repeat the incident from the book: He goes into more depth to explain *why* the incident was funny.

You can use the same principle for writing book reports about nonfiction. If information makes you scared, mad, or upset, explain why. Then explain how the author brought you to that point:

I felt very angry while reading *Save the Whales* because I began to understand that these beautiful creatures are really in danger. The author helps build up these feelings. First, she shows you how beautiful and majestic whales are. She really makes you see the awesome sight of a huge whale spouting off. She describes in great detail the way whales care for their babies. By the time you find out how many of these creatures are killed each year, you really care about them.

The writer of the paragraph above starts out saying she felt angry. Then she explains why: She is upset that whales are endangered. Finally, she goes into more depth, explaining how the author's arguments lead up to these feelings. The author shows the reader that whales are beautiful, majestic, and care for their babies. That's how the author gets the reader to care about the whales. The writer of the paragraph explains exactly *how* the author got her to care about the whales, which gives her report more depth.

Unusual Formats for Book Reports

Maybe your teacher has asked you to find an unusual format for a book report—or maybe you're the one getting tired of the same old thing. In either case, some of these ideas may give you a fresh slant on how to understand and express your feelings for a book. If your teacher has not assigned them, however, be sure to get permission to write your report in any of the following ways.

Write a letter from one of the characters in the book to another, or have one of the characters write a letter to you or to someone you know. This can be a wonderful way to get to know a character better. Thinking about what the character is concerned about helps you understand who the character is and what he or she is doing in the book. Having different characters write to each other can help you understand their relationship. Having a character write to you can help bring out your feelings about a character. If your character writes to someone you know, it might give you the freedom to play in your writing, exploring both your feelings about the character and your feelings about the person you know.

Be a reader from Mars reporting on this book to your planet. The book you read may seem familiar to you. However, what would it look like to someone from a whole other world? What do you take for granted that might look strange to another person? What do you interpret one way that someone else might interpret differently? For example, you understand that a hug usually means that one person likes another. However, would someone from another planet think that a hug meant that one person was trying to hold another person's arms in order not to get hit? Thinking about different ways of looking at the same thing can help you realize what you take for granted—and things about your own thinking that you would like to shake up or change. Thinking about what a book might mean to somebody else can help you realize what it means to you.

Be a reader from another time, in the past or future, reporting on this book. This kind of report serves a similar purpose to the ''reader from Mars'' report, with the added advantage that it helps you to think about another time. Imagining how a book would look to a reader from the past helps you think about the past. In earlier times, people made different assumptions than we do today. Trying to get inside that way of thinking as you write about the book helps you understand both the past and your own time better. Imagining how a book would look to a reader from the future lets your imagination go. What do you think the future will be like? How will it be different from the present? Will some things be better? Will other things be worse? Thinking about the future gives you another perspective on the present.

Introduce the main character of this book to a friend of yours by letter. What would you say to your friend about this character? If you pretend your friend is an employer, why should he or she hire this character? If you pretend your friend is moving to another city and might like to look this character up, why might your friend like to do this? Would this character be a good friend to your friend? Maybe the character is a villain and you want to warn your friend to watch out. Imagining the character in another situation than the ones in the book helps you to understand the book better.

Be a movie director or television producer writing a letter to the studio or network. Argue why this book would make a great show. Explain what scenes you would emphasize; which, if any, you would cut out; and what stars might play the lead. In this report, you have to think about the book as a whole, not just one character in it. By relating it to another medium, you have to think about the way it works as a book. Some scenes may work well when you read about them but be hard to film. Other scenes may have reminded you of a dramatic movie or television show because of all the action. Perhaps some characters reminded you of your favorite stars. These feelings can be expressed in a report of this kind.

Write your own story, poem, or play, based on characters or events in this book. Have you ever wished that an author would keep right on going, past the ending, or that two characters from different parts of the book, or from different books, could meet each other? Would you like to imagine the character in a different setting, such as in your own home? Or would you like to imagine what you would do if you could enter the world of the book and be friends with some of the characters there? Let your imagination go. Write a story, play, or poem telling what happens after the ending, or in another part of the story that the author didn't tell, or if your world and the character's world met somehow. You can be a writer as well as a reader!

Write a poem telling how the book made you feel. Sometimes a book stirs deep feelings that you don't want to think about. Instead, you just want to feel. Writing a report means thinking about your feelings, analyzing and discussing them, and explaining how the book brought them up. Writing a poem means finding the words to express just exactly how you felt, either directly or through images or a story. Sometimes it's important to analyze your feelings— but other times, a poem can be the best way to say what you mean.

Do an art project. Make a model of a scene from the book, draw illustrations from it, and design clothes for the characters; or make a picture that expresses your feelings about the book. Some people think better in pictures than in words, and some books just cry out to be shown in pictures. If you're one of those people or if this is one of those books, your teacher might accept an art project as your way of explaining what you thought of the book and what it meant to you.

Whichever format you use to write a book report, remember that in the end *you're* the person you should satisfy with your report. Think about what you have learned from the book and about yourself from reading it. Understanding your own feelings and then relating them to another person are important skills. Knowing how to read, having access to the different worlds that books can open, and understanding what an author is trying to do are likewise important. The more you understand how a book is affecting you, the more you will be able to decide what you think of it and whether you would recommend it to someone else. Writing book reports doesn't have to be a difficult or painful experience. Instead, it can be a way for you to learn, grow, and be entertained—and then share those experiences with others.

Index